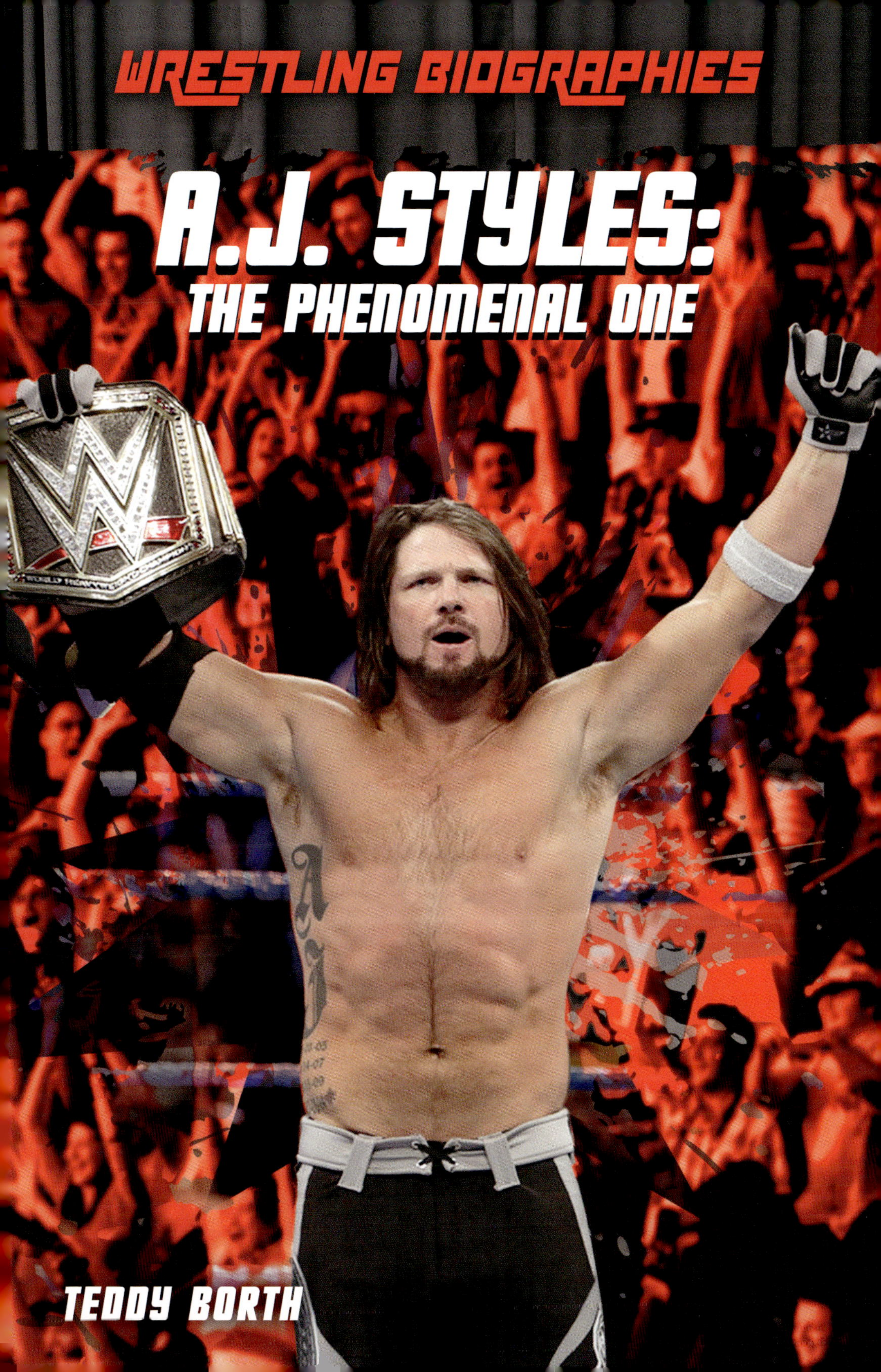
WRESTLING BIOGRAPHIES
A.J. STYLES:
THE PHENOMENAL ONE
TEDDY BORTH

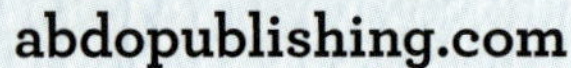

abdopublishing.com

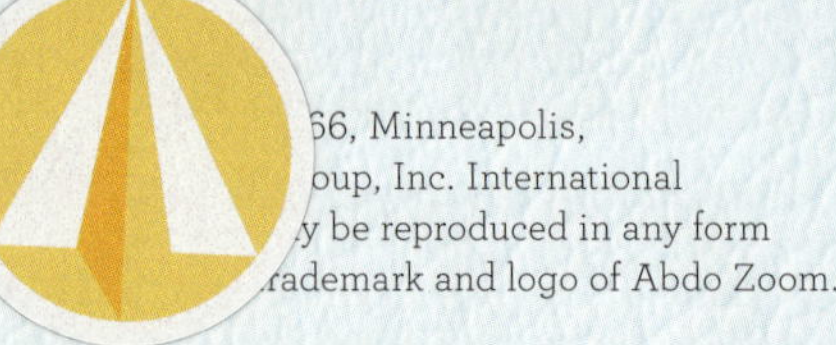

Printed in the United States of America, North Mankato, Minnesota.
092017
012018

Photo Credits: Alamy, AllWrestlingSuperstars.com, AP Images, Getty Images, Icon Sportswire, iStock, Seth Poppel/Yearbook Library, Shutterstock
Production Contributors: Kenny Abdo, Jennie Forsberg, Grace Hansen
Design Contributors: Dorothy Toth, Neil Klinepier

Publisher's Cataloging-in-Publication Data

Names: Borth, Teddy, author.
Title: A.J. Styles: the phenomenal one / by Teddy Borth.
Other titles: The phenomenal one
Description: Minneapolis, Minnesota: Abdo Zoom, 2018. Series: Wrestling biographies | Includes online resource and index.
Identifiers: LCCN 2017939283 | ISBN 9781532121067 (lib.bdg.) ISBN 9781532122187 (ebook) | ISBN 9781532122743 (Read-to-Me ebook)
Subjects: LCSH: Styles, A.J.(Allen Jones), d1977- --Juvenile literature. Wrestlers--Juvenile literature. | Biography--Juvenile literature.
Classification: DDC 796.812 [B]--dc23
LC record available at https://lccn.loc.gov/2017939283

TABLE OF CONTENTS

EARLY LIFE

A.J. Styles was born Allen Neal Jones. He was born on June 2, 1977 in Jacksonville, North Carolina.

Styles never watched wrestling growing up. He only got into it because his friends were trying it. He quickly found he was good at it.

INDEPENDENT WRESTLER

After some training, Styles debuted in 1998. He joined National Championship Wrestling. After one year, he was the champion of NCW.

KEVIN
STEEN
AJ
STYLES

Styles made his WWE debut in 2002. They offered him a **contract**. He turned it down. The time wasn't right.

TNA

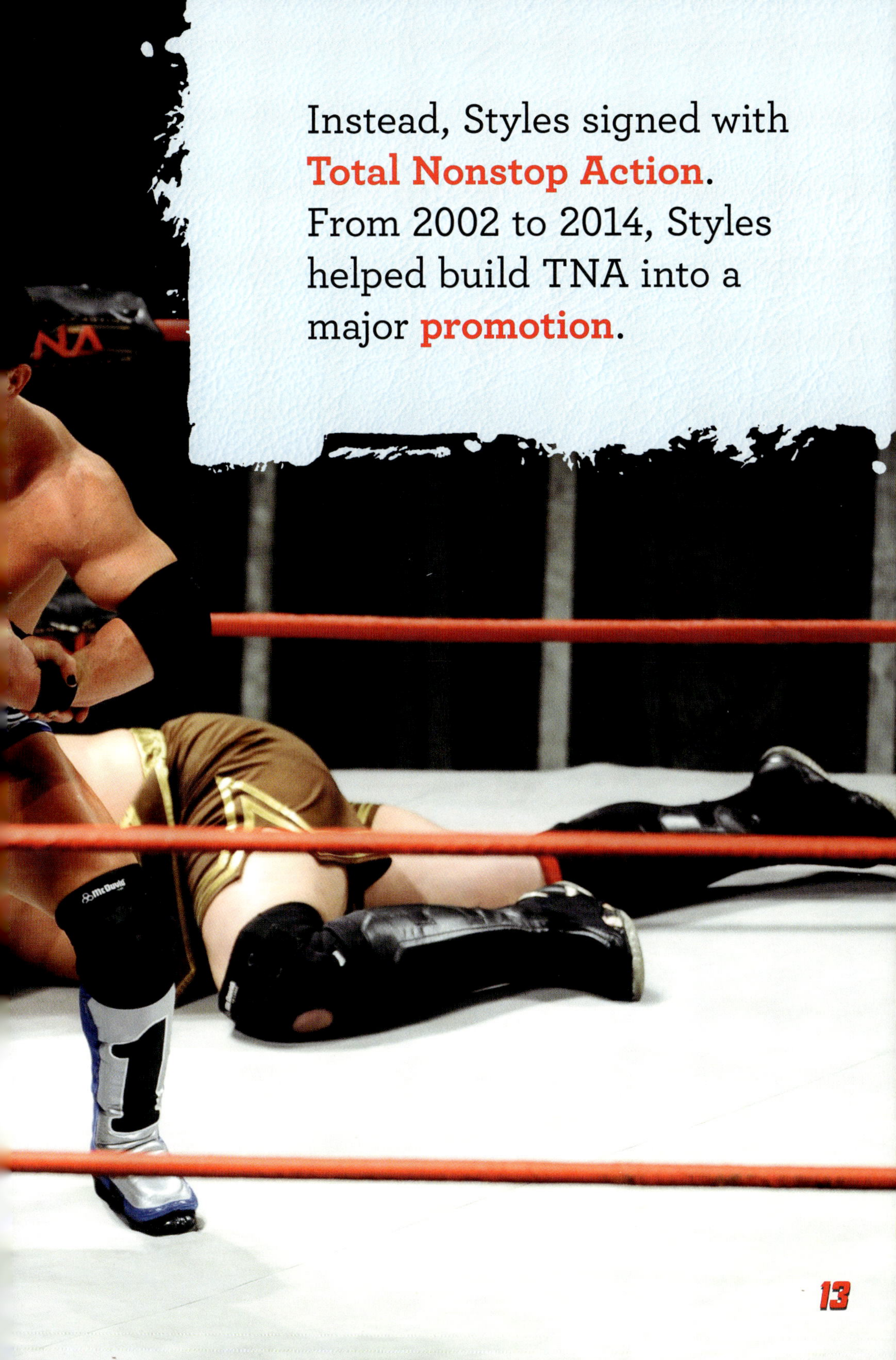

Instead, Styles signed with **Total Nonstop Action**. From 2002 to 2014, Styles helped build TNA into a major **promotion**.

Styles

Styles was called the face of **TNA**. Through them, he was able to compete around the world. He wrestled in places like Mexico and Japan.

FREE AGENT

Styles had made an impact. He was called one of the best wrestlers in the world. In 2014, he was wrestling's hottest **free agent**.

AJ

Styles made a return to New Japan Pro Wrestling. There, he became a top **villain**. He also spent time wrestling in many other **promotions**.

RETURN TO WWE

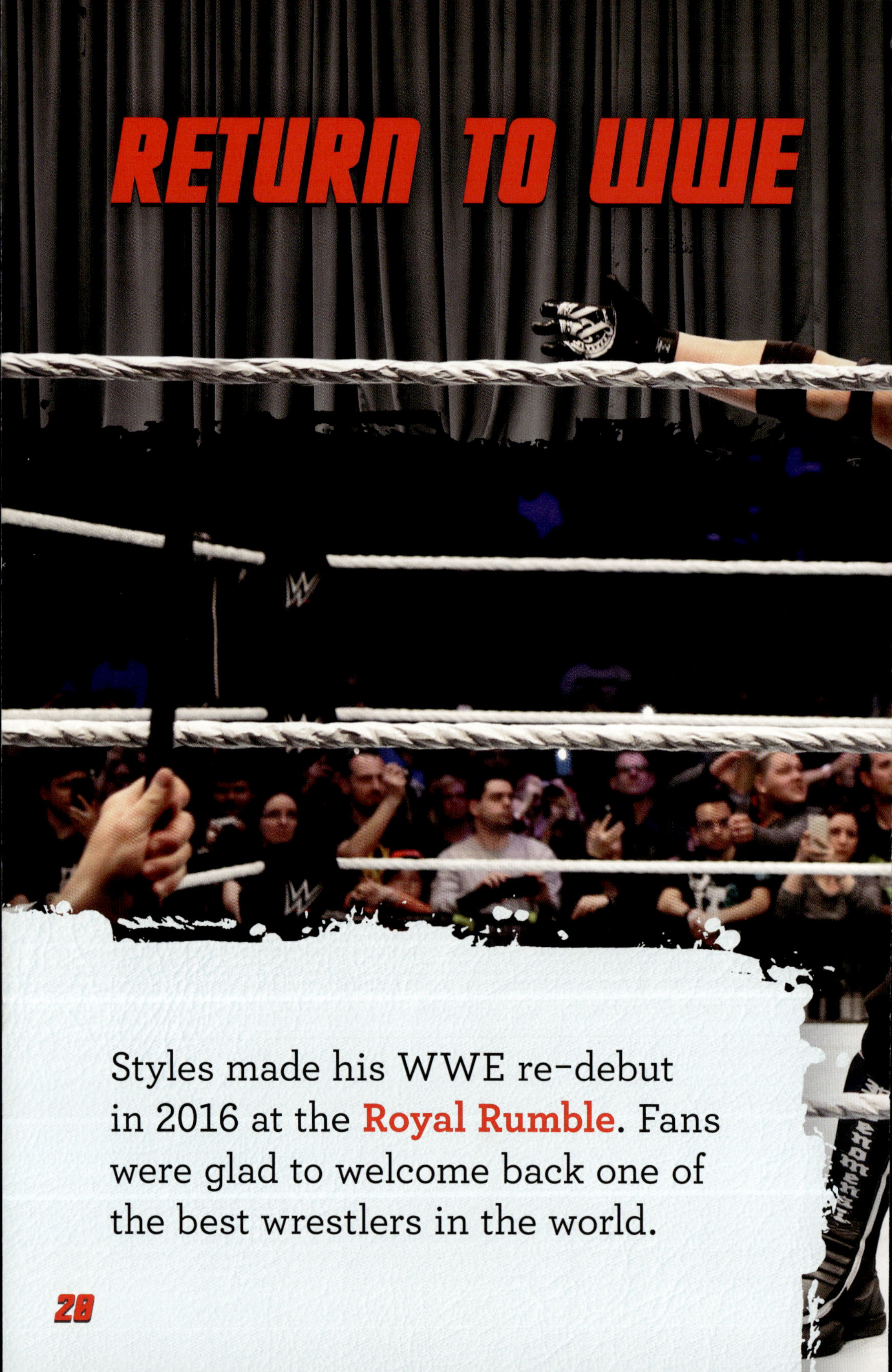

Styles made his WWE re-debut in 2016 at the **Royal Rumble**. Fans were glad to welcome back one of the best wrestlers in the world.

GLOSSARY

contract – an agreement between a company and wrestler that they are going to work together.

free agent – a person not exclusive to one company. They are able to work for anyone.

promotion – in wrestling, a company that puts on regular wrestling shows. WWE, TNA, and New Japan Pro Wrestling are examples of wrestling promotions.

Royal Rumble – a major WWE show held every year in January.

TNA – Total Nonstop Action is a wrestling company in the United States. In 2017, it changed to Global Force Wrestling.

villain – a person who is intentionally evil and cheats to win the match.

ONLINE RESOURCES

Booklinks
NONFICTION NETWORK
FREE! ONLINE NONFICTION RESOURCES

To learn more about A.J. Styles, please visit **abdobooklinks.com**. These links are routinely monitored and updated to provide the most current information available.

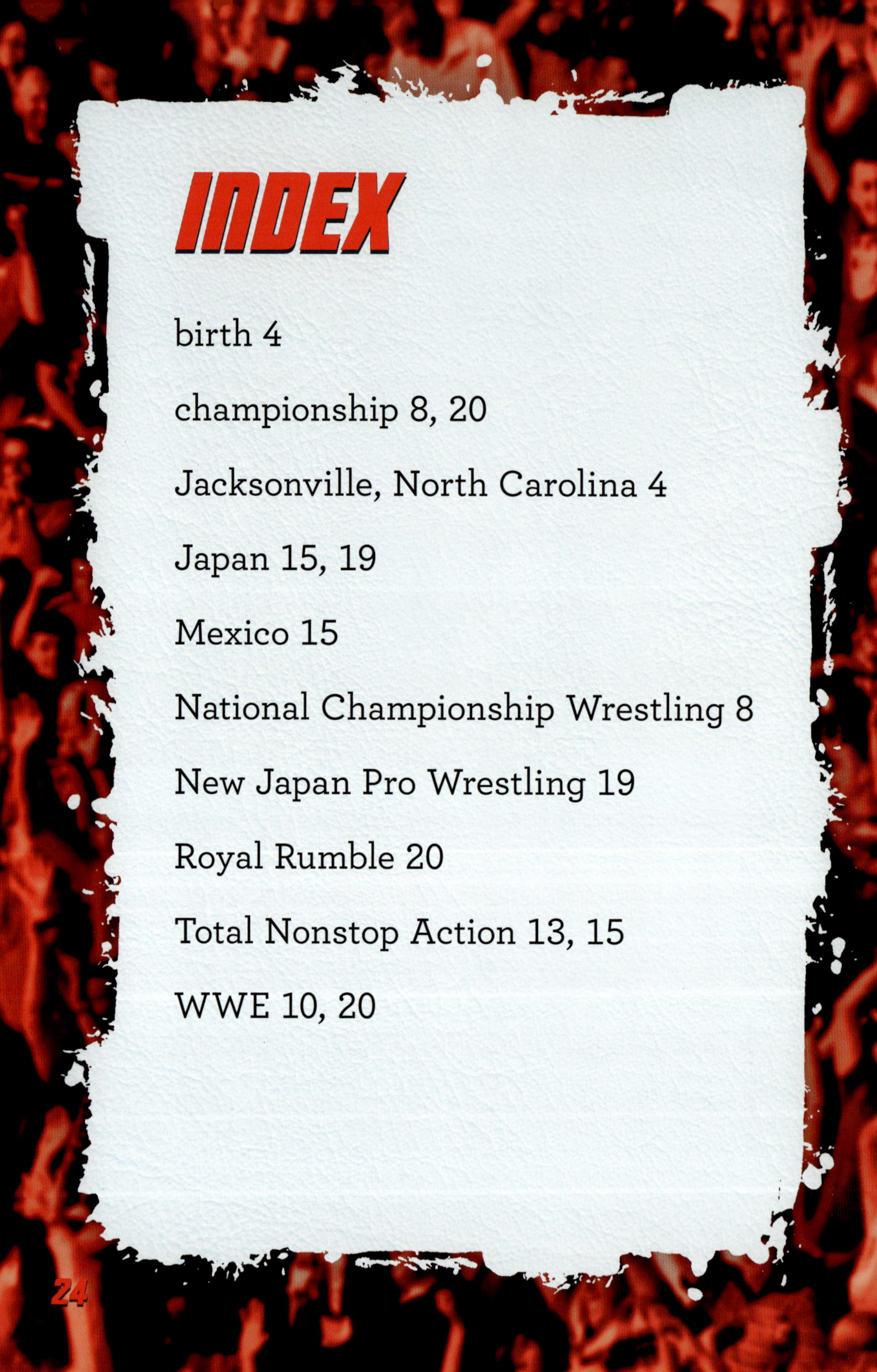

INDEX